HISTORY ENCYCLOPEDIA
PROMINENT CIVILISATIONS

An imprint of Om Books International

Contents

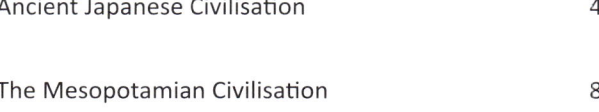

Ancient Japanese Civilisation	4
The Mesopotamian Civilisation	8
Ancient Egyptian Civilisation	12
Mayan Civilisation	14
Harappa and Mohenjo Daro Communities	16
Aryan Migration	17
Hinduism and Vedic Period	18
Rise of Jainism	19
Jain Tirthankaras	20
Rise of Buddhism	21
Principles of Buddhism	22
Spread of Buddha's Word	23
The Mauryan Dynasty	24
Persian Empire	25
The Vikings – A Warrior Civilisation	26
Chinese Civilisation	28
The Inca Civilisation	31

Prominent Civilisations, Dynasties and Religions

3000 BCE–1707 CE

The Indus Valley Civilisation was one of the oldest civilisations to flourish in Asia. Existing around 2500 BCE, this civilisation flourished along the flood plains of the Indus river in present day Pakistan and northwest India. People belonging to the Indus valley civilisation, also known as Dravidians, had a prosperous commerce and trade industry. By around 1700 BCE, the civilisation began to decline.

Many other civilisations, such as the Chinese, Persian and Egyptian give us a glimpse into the lives of people in bygone eras, their politics, religion and way of life. Many of these are well recorded and we have visible evidence of those periods. This period also saw the birth of prominent religions like Buddhism and Jainism.

HISTORY ENCYCLOPEDIA

Ancient Japanese Civilisation

Right from 50,000 BCE, indigenous tribes occupied Japan. It was only around 12,000 BCE that the Ice Age brought about the end of the Paleolithic Age in Japan. Different periods marked the history of ancient Japan, each leaving behind a legacy that impacted the culture of the Japan that we know today.

Jomon Period

The period of time from 13,000 BCE to approximately 300 BCE is known as the Jomon Period to historians. This essentially encompasses Japan's Neolithic period. It was known for its pottery and ceramics, which had a unique "cord marked" pattern. The word "Jomon", in fact, represents these cord-like patterns. It is believed that the Jomon people were semi-sedentary and obtained their food through hunting, fishing and gathering.

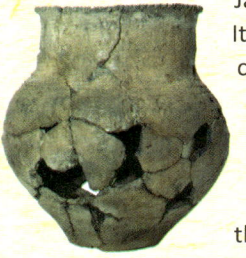
Remains from the Jomon period

Yayoi Period

The Jomon Period was followed by the Yayoi Period, which flourished from 300 BCE to 250 CE. During this period, Japan began using metals like bronze and iron. People also discovered newer techniques of agriculture (wet rice cultivation) and weaving. They began to live in permanent communities and clusters of thatched houses.

Kofun Period

The documented history of Japan starts with the Kofun Period from about 250 CE to around 538 CE. It got its name from the Kofun burial grounds that were discovered in Tanegashima Island located to the south of Kyushu. The Shinto culture prevailed during this period and still exists in Japan.

Sumo wrestling is an ancient Japanese art which originated in the Shinto religion.

A famous Shinto shrine.

Asuka Period

The Asuka period existed from about 552 CE to 645 CE. This period was characterised by its strong administration, clear boundaries and trade ties with South Korea. It also marked the beginning of Buddhism. The rulers, Empress Suiko and Prince Shotoku, spread the teachings of Buddha. Other ideas that appeared during this time were the documenting of history, using coins as currency, standardising weights and measures, and a central bureaucratic Government.

Nara Period

Also known as the Golden Era of Japanese history, the Nara period extended from 710 CE to 782 CE. It was named after the city of Nara, which became the base of culture and political power. This period saw its people settled in villages and focussed primarily on agriculture. But the establishment was overtaken by greed and imposed heavy taxes, leading to protest and unrest during the closing decades of this period.

Heian Period

The capital moved from Nara to Heian-kyo (known as Kyoto today) in 794 CE. This was followed by almost 400 years of peace, overseen by the aristocratic Fujiwara family, who dominated both politics and culture. An awareness of their own heritage led the Japanese to express themselves in both literature and art. The kana script, which became the Japanese writing system; the waka style of poetry; the monogatari, or narrative tales; and nikki, or diaries, evolved during this period.

Kamakura Period

The feudal era came into play during the Kamakura Period (1192–1333 CE). It was during this period that the Samurai class came to power. The royalty became figureheads with the real power being vested in the samurai, shogun and military aristocracy. Mongol invasions in 1274 and 1281 drained the economy, which heralded the disintegration of this period.

The painted Japanese fan is indicative of the delicate artistry prevalent in Japan.

The samurai warriors of ancient Japan.

Muromachi Period

The period that followed, that is, the Muromachi Period (1392–1573) saw economic and artistic revival, and economic progress. Transportation and urban development were the key themes of this period. Zen Buddhism made an appearance and impacted all aspects of life – art, commerce, education and politics. Kyoto became the hub of power once again. The shoguns built elegant villas and performed the elaborate tea ceremony. Garden designs, architecture, flower arrangements, calligraphy and preparing and serving food gained much importance. The Noh dance drama, a slow and elaborate performance, also gained popularity.

The tea ceremony is an elaborate ritual that takes years to master.

The Noh dance drama.

Azuchi-Momoyama Period

The internal conflicts of Japan came to an end with the Azuchi-Momoyama period. By the beginning of the sixteenth century, Christian Missionaries made an advent, but they were not too successful with conversions. This was followed by the Edo period (1603–1868) where Japan began to isolate itself from the rest of the world in terms of trade and missionaries, largely due to the fear of European invasion.

The Kabuki – an ancient dance form

The Kabuki dance form first was seen during the early seventeenth century. It is believed that a female dancer called Okuni would perform with wandering troupes of female performers. Women were banned from performing this dance during 1629. For a while, young boys, dressed as women, performed. Finally, in the eighteenth century, it was accepted again. It depicted historical events and grand love stories. The Kabuki is famous for its elaborate costumes and subtle movements.

Kabuki originated in the seventeenth century in Kyoto. It is still widely performed in Japan.

PROMINENT CIVILISATIONS

Martial arts

The martial arts are deeply connected with Japan's history. Ancient Japan saw much conflict. With the Samurai playing a significant role, ancient Japanese were great students of weaponry and combat techniques. Over a period of time, they developed martial arts into a science, backing it up with deep study. From the twelfth century, combat techniques began to be formalised. Even today, many Japanese martial art forms are practiced. Kyūdō, or the art of archery; Sōjutsu and Naginatajutsu, or combat with the spear; and Kenjutsu or sword fighting were among some of the martial arts that held sway. Judo is yet another form that is practiced even today, though it finds its origins in Jujutsu. The most popular form, Karate, is believed to have originated from Okinawa, where natives would simply call this form "te".

Karate, an ancient martial art, is widely practiced even today.

Historical attire

The Kimono first came into existence during the Jomon period, when there was no great difference between what men and women wore. The word kimono literally means "thing to wear". As trading with the outside world began, newer ways of wearing clothes made an appearance. Until the fifteenth century, people wore kimonos that were made of hemp or linen. Traditionally, the art of wearing a kimono was passed on from mother to daughter. Today, this art is also taught in schools. Western clothing was first adopted by soldiers of the shogun's army and navy, who found the style more flexible and convenient.

The kimono is a traditional Japanese dress worn by women, that is popular even today.

FUN FACT

Sushi, a popular Japanese dish, needs to be made delicately. It is said that the blade of a professional sushi chef needs to be sharpened every day – just like the sword of a samurai.

HISTORY ENCYCLOPEDIA

The Mesopotamian Civilisation

The name Mesopotamia is derived from the Greek language and means "between rivers". This basically refers to the land that lies between the rivers of Tigris and Euphrates. However, in reality, Mesopotamia includes areas that are more commonly known as eastern Syria, southeastern Turkey and a large part of Iraq today. The Mesopotamian civilisation is the longest one in history and is known for giving birth to many of the European states that we see today.

Relief of an ancient assyrian king.

Establishing boundaries

The first evidence of people occupying this land goes back to 6000 BCE, when early settlers built villages in Northern Assyria. As the population grew, the area began to get politically divided into smaller independent "city-states". This was followed by a forced unification under the rule of King Lugal-zage-si of Uruk (a city in ancient Sumer). In 2000 BCE, the country was divided into smaller units once again, after repeated wars. Finally, Babylon established a state in the south and Assyria, in the north. Assyria went on to build an empire that, for a period, consisted the entire ancient Middle East. This remained steady under various Neo-Babylonian and Persian kings, up to Alexander the Great's conquests in 331 BCE.

Religion through the years

Mesopotamia, as a region, was influenced by many different cultures and invasions. Despite these, it maintained a tradition of its own. Nature was worshipped along with deities that appeared to meet different kinds of needs, such as power, fertility, wealth, etc. Slowly, concepts like sin and forgiveness also made an appearance.

Literature of Mesopotamia

Mesopotamian literature is possibly the oldest known literature in the world. The literary evidence provides a storehouse of information in the form of clay tablets inscribed with texts written in cuneiform script.

The ancient city of Babylon.

PROMINENT CIVILISATIONS

Key themes included religious texts, hymns, prayers, incantations, descriptions of rituals, etc. Many songs and stories talk about life in that period. There is evidence of legal or medical texts. As writing became more precise through the third millennium BCE, a considerable body of literature found its way into written form. Much of this found its way into Sumerian scribal schools, indicating an organised education system. Mesopotamian literature abounded in myths, laments, prayers and stories of war and bravery.

Writing of the ancient Sumerian or Assyrian civilisation.

Major achievements

Mathematics and astronomy flowered during this period. Some concepts used even today include the sexagesimal system to calculate time and angles; the 12 "double-hours" Greek day; the zodiac, sunsigns, etc. The Pythogoras law, though credited to Greek mathematician Pythogoras, made an appearance in early Babylonian tablets during 1900–1600 BCE, indicating a knowledge of this logic. Legal theory during this period also flourished and much of it was documented in various collections termed as "codes" by historians.

The most famous of these is the "Code of Hammurabi". These codes focussed on concern for the weak, widows, orphans, etc.

Changing life over centuries

Buildings were made of mud-brick and were thus vulnerable to weather vagaries; over centuries, layers of settlement created mounds that characterised the ruins of Mesopotamia. Over the centuries, life in ancient Mesopotamia underwent changes. Humans moved from a nomadic to sedentary life. This was followed by the emergence of an agricultural economy with deliberate farming methods. The erection of permanent houses, temples and burial grounds indicated the organisation of society. Specialised craft, division of labour, use of new materials like metals were indicative of the transition from the late Neolithic to a Chalcolithic period.

Bee-hive houses in Mesopotamia (present-day Turkey).

FAST FACT

In the Mesopotamian religion, people believed that after death, everybody would become a ghost.

HISTORY ENCYCLOPEDIA

Tablet with cuneiform script

3500 BCE
The evolution of writing begins. At first, it appears in the form of pictograms, but takes about a thousand years to evolve into a full cuneiform script.

The Code of Ur-Nammu, the first complete law code.

2100 BCE
The city of Ur becomes the centre of a powerful Mesopotamian state. It soon falls into decline. This marks the decline of the Sumerians as the Amorites, a nomadic people, start moving into Mesopotamia.

5000-3500 BCE
Sumerians set up the first city states in southern Mesopotamia.

Map of Babylonia, Mesopotamia.

2300 BCE
King Sargon of Akkad starts conquering the first empire in world history. The empire reaches its height in 2220 BCE.

Statue of King Sargon.

PROMINENT CIVILISATIONS

King Cyrus at a Babylonian temple.

1530 BCE
Babylonia is conquered by the Kassites, who rule the area for 400+ years.

Portrait of an old Chaldean man.

1100 BCE
Nomadic peoples such as the Aramaeans and the Chaldeans over run much of Mesopotamia. The kingdoms of Babylon and Assyria go into temporary decline.

1792-49 BCE
King Hammurabi of Babylon conquers a large empire. Hammurabi is famous for the law code which he issues. His empire begins to decline immediately after his death.

Law code of Hammurabi.

1500 BCE
The Mitanni (Indo-European people) conquer northern Mesopotamia and areas of Syria and Asia Minor. After 200 years, the kingdom of Assyria conquers northern Mesopotamia from the Mitanni.

Map of Syria.

Ancient Egyptian Civilisation

The ancient Egyptian civilisation is one of the longest civilisations in human history. It lasted for more than 3000 years from 3150 BCE to 30 BCE. Today, Egypt is a small country in the north-eastern corner of Africa. Yet, its history is great and powerful. The monuments and tombs of the Pharaohs of Egypt, called pyramids, which are over 4000 years old, continue to stand even today. Till date, over 130 pyramids have been discovered in Egypt.

The Great Nile

The River Nile, the longest river in the world, flows through Egypt. A land of deserts, barely receiving any rainfall, Egypt would have been a barren land, had it not been for the Nile. The river allowed the ancient Egyptian civilisation to thrive and flourish. Every year, the rain in southern Africa would cause the Nile to flood. However, the floods brought in the rich soil of the mountainsides, causing the land to be extremely fertile. Naturally the vegetation in Egypt thrived, giving life to its civilisation.

Earlier, Egypt was made of two kingdoms, on either side of the Nile. In the 3rd millennium BCE BCE, Pharaoh Menes conquered the other kingdom and Egypt was united.

Practices of the afterlife

The afterlife was very important to the Egyptians. They preserved their dead bodies by mummifying them. The bodies of the dead would be oiled and their internal organs would be removed. The bodies would then be wrapped in long strips of cloth. The dead were buried with their personal belongings, which the Egyptians believed would be needed in the afterlife.

The Pharaohs were given a more elaborate burial. Pyramids were built for them, where they would be buried with all their riches. Over the centuries, many objects have been retrieved from the pyramids. The wall paintings on the tombs have also depicted the daily lives of ancient Egyptians.

An Egyptian mummy.

FAST FACT

The Pharaoh always covered his head as his hair was not to be seen by regular people.

Pyramids of Egypt.

Royal temples

The rulers of Egypt considered themselves to be gods and built temples in their honour, celebrating important events during their reign. For example, in Queen Hatshepsut's temple, a wall relief depicts her expedition by sea.

Ruins of the Hatshepsut temple, Egypt.

Gods and Goddesses

Apart from royalty, the Egyptians worshipped several gods and goddesses and built temples in their honour. The most important God was Ra, the Sun God. He had the head of a hawk and a headdress with a sun disk. Other important gods were Isis, Osiris, Horus and Thoth.

Egyptian writings

The alphabet of the ancient Egyptians was in the form of pictures, called hieroglyphics. The Egyptian alphabet contained more than 700 hieroglyphs. Some of the symbols represented sounds, while some depicted entire words.

Hieroglyphic carvings on the walls of an ancient Egyptian temple.

Games and entertainment

The Egyptians enjoyed various activities for entertainment. Festivals and games were an important part of their daily lives. They enjoyed hunting, board games, storytelling, swimming, archery, wrestling, chariot racing, dancing, as well as playing with toys.

FAST FACT

Cats were considered sacred in Ancient Egypt. The house cat was a symbol of grace and poise.

Mayan Civilisation

The Mayan civilisation primarily existed in and around the lowlands of the area that is present-day Guatemala. It was at the pinnacle of its existence during the sixth century CE. The Maya are believed to have been an advanced people and were known for their hieroglyphic writing, mathematics, pottery, agricultural techniques and calendar-making. They left behind a stunning body of work that has helped us learn about their skills, way of life, religion and politics.

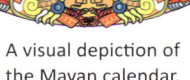

A visual depiction of the Mayan calendar.

Evolution

The earliest known Mayan settlements have been said to exist around 1500 CE. Over the next several centuries, till about 300 CE, the Maya extended their influence across both highlands and lowlands.

The Golden Age of the Mayan civilisation began approximately around 250 CE. During this period, the Maya built over 40 cities, each with a population ranging from 5000 to 50,000 people. At its height, the Mayan population is believed to have crossed 2,000,000 people.

Architecture

The Mayan cities had names like Tikal, Uaxactún, Copán, Bonampak, Dos Pilas, Calakmul, Palenque and Río Bec. These cities were surrounded and supported by agricultural communities and villages. The Maya followed modern techniques of agriculture like terracing and irrigation, which can be seen from the remains of their cities. The evidence of the architectural brilliance and advanced imagination of the Maya is visible in the palaces, pyramids, temples and plazas that have been discovered during archaeological excavations.

A pyramidical temple from the Maya period.

PROMINENT CIVILISATIONS

Religion

The Maya had deep religious beliefs. They prayed to many Gods and their Gods were especially related to nature. These included sun, moon, rain and corn Gods. The importance of art in Mayan life and religion is evident from the detailed work on their many temples and palaces. Many temples were pyramidical and decorated with inscriptions and relief work.

While evidence has already proven that they were great thinkers, the Maya also made strides in mathematics and astronomy – including the use of zero. They also developed a detailed calendar, with 365 days. Another significant discovery was the discovery of the system of hieroglyphic writing. The Maya used paper made from tree bark. They converted this paper to books known as codices. Four codices have survived over time, which have helped us discover more information about the Mayan way of life.

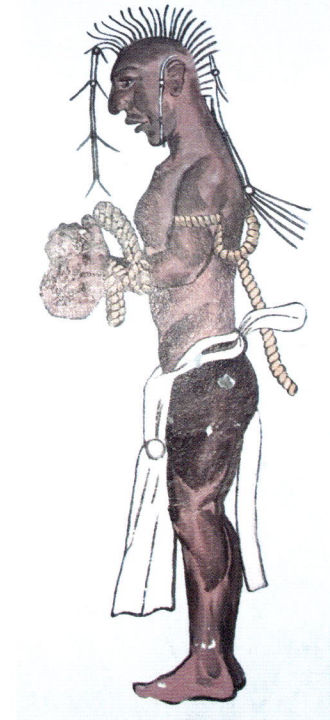
The typical clothes of a Mayan man.

Attire

The Maya were well-known for their use of colourful clothes as well as the unusual body modifications they created. Based on the material available to them, the Maya had a wide variety of clothes for different occasions—elaborate costumes for ceremonies, vibrant dance outfits, elaborate armour for protection and simple flexible clothes for everyday wear. During public events that were attended by large crowds, the ruling class would wear elaborate headdresses, jewellery made of jade and clothes made from the skin of animals that were considered to be "dangerous". This elaborate attire was a mark of their own status and power.

For everyday wear, most of the Mayan people wore a simple outfit that usually comprised a loin cloth or a short skirt for men; and a long skirt for women. These were elaborately embellished with jewellery like bracelets, anklets and neck pieces. Their hair was almost never left loose; it was often tied together with bands and decorated with feathers.

Decline

The Mayan civilisation flourished extremely well, which is why historians feel that its disintegration appears to be a mystery. Between the eighth and ninth century, many Mayan cities were abandoned and the reason behind this event remains unknown even today. By 900 CE, the Mayan civilisation had virtually collapsed.

Use of natural resources

A factor that has both mystified and amazed historians is the ability of the Mayan people to create such a large, thriving civilisation in the inhospitable rainforest regions, which is where this civilisation flourished.

When one sees the history of ancient civilisations, it can be observed that most of them existed in drier climates, mainly because they did not have the technology to battle elements. This perhaps worked in favour of the Mayan people, for many foreign invaders left the Maya to their own devices, finding the climate unfavourable with no marked riches, silver and gold to attract them. However, the Maya made the most of the natural resources available to them. They used limestone for construction, volcanic rock deposits for making tools, and jade, quetzal feathers, etc., for decorating royal costumes and shells as trumpets during formal ceremonies, as well as war.

Statue of a Mayan god.

> **FAST FACT**
>
> The Maya had advanced medical practices. They are known to have performed surgery and made artificial limbs with jade and turquoise; they even used human hair for suturing.

Harappa and Mohenjo Daro Communities

The Indus Valley Civilisation spanned across different parts of India, such as present-day Punjab, Haryana, Sindh, Baluchistan, Gujarat and Uttar Pradesh. Artefacts from this civilisation show that its inhabitants followed a number system. This civilisation was perhaps the first of the settlements in the Indian subcontinent. Cities such as Mohenjo Daro and Harappa also had citadels (fortress above a city), proper drainage and sewage system.

Mould of a seal, Indus Valley Civilisation (2500–1700 BCE).

Life of the people

The people of the Indus Valley Civilisation subsisted on farming. They reared cattle, pigs, sheep and goats. They also practised hunting and fishing. They grew wheat, cotton, chickpeas, mustard and sesame among other crops. They also traded gold, copper and silver.

Archaeologists have found several toys during the excavations, such as toy carts, rattles, whistles, pull-along animals, etc. The toys were made of clay and terracotta. They also played dice games and board games. Evidence suggests that they enjoyed the sport of cock-fighting. The seals found in the Indus valley show us how the men and women dressed. The men wore loincloths and women wore dresses. Both men and women wore jewellery, such as beads.

They traded goods, such as pots, gems like turquoise, seashells, gold and silver. They also knew the craft of building boats. Indus valley seals have been found in Mesopotamia. This suggests that they had trade relations with Mesopotamia.

Evidence of writing

Artefacts, such as seals found at these sites, prove that the people from this civilisation were literate. Unfortunately, the Indus Valley writing has still not been deciphered. The writing has around 400 picture symbols.

Ruins of Mohenjo Daro, Pakistan.

PROMINENT CIVILISATIONS

Aryan Migration

The word Aryan is derived from the Sanskrit word Arya, meaning noble. It was also used to refer to the Indo-Iranian tribes that lived during the prehistoric times in ancient Iran and the Indian subcontinent. Today, the word "Aryan" is used as part of the term "Indo-Aryan languages in South Asia."

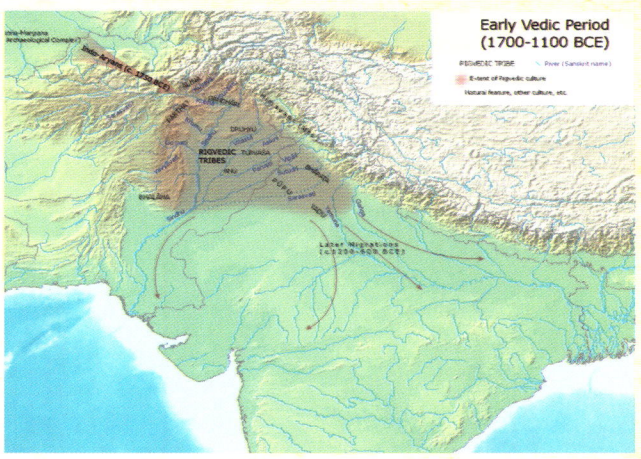

Map showing early vedic India and the extent of the Aryan migration.

Indo-Aryan migration theory

In the nineteenth century, German linguist and Sanskrit scholar, Max Muller, proposed the Indo-Aryan migration theory when a similarity between European and Indian languages was discovered.

The theory suggests that the Indo-Aryan group of languages were introduced in the Indian subcontinent when people from central Asia, that is, the Indo-Iranians migrated here around 1800 BCE and brought the Indo-Aryan languages with them.

The Indo-Aryan languages are a part of the Indo-European group of languages. The theory aims to explain how the Indo-European languages developed and spread over different parts of the world. Thus, the theory is a meeting point of archaeological, anthropological and linguistic research.

Migration to India

The Aryan migration is believed to have occurred during the Indus valley civilisation. Coming from Central Asia, these large groups of nomadic cattle herders crossed the Hindu Kush mountains.

In fact, some researchers believe that this settling down near the Indus valley civilisation could be one of the reasons for its collapse.

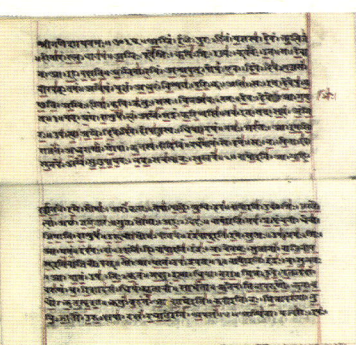

Rig veda was written during the Vedic period somewhere between 1500 and 1000 BCE.

Illustration of Aryans entering India during the Indus Valley Civilisation.

FAST FACT

It is theorised that the language of the Aryans soon gained popularity over the local languages and they too turned to agriculture to survive. There is, however, mention of the Aryans in the Vedas, the Indian religious books that contain stories of struggles and conflicts.

Hinduism and Vedic Period

Hinduism does not have a particular founder or a particular date of origin. Hinduism refers to many different beliefs, philosophies and perspectives that originated in India. It is also called the Sanatana dharma. It is a polytheistic religion, that is, it involves worship of several gods.

Hazarar Rama temple, Hampi, Karnataka, India.

Temple in Karnataka state, India.

Vedic period

The word Hindu is derived from the Sanskrit word "Sindhu", which was the name given to the river Indus by the Persians. The Indus valley civilisation was followed by the Vedic period (1500–500 BCE) during which an emphasis on religious sacrifice or yajnas and other religious rituals began to gain prominence.

The Vedic period saw the worship of various Gods, such as Indra, Vayu, Marut, Varun, Rudra, Agni, etc. During this period, the Vedas were written in Vedic Sanskrit. They are ancient texts that contain Hindu teachings. The word Veda means knowledge in Sanskrit. The Vedas were compiled by Vyasa Krishna Dwaipayana around 1500 BCE.

The four Vedas

There are four Vedas: the Rigveda, the Yajurveda, the Samaveda and the Atharvaveda. Collectively the four Vedas are known as Chathur Veda.

The Vedas are called Shruti, that is, which need to be heard. While other religious texts are called Smriti, that is, which need to be memorised.

Each Veda has four parts. The primary section is the mantra or hymn section, also known as Samhitas, next are the Brahmanas containing commentaries on rituals, followed by the Aranyakas explaining rituals and sacrifices. The Upanishads discuss philosophy and meditation.

The Rigveda means Veda of praise. It is supposed to be the main Veda. It contains 1028 hymns or suktas and 10,600 verses and is divided into 10 mandalas or books. The Samaveda means the Veda of sacred songs. It is a collection of melodies. The Yajurveda means the Veda of sacrifice. It explains various mantras to be sung and religious rituals to be followed by priests. The Atharvaveda means the Veda of the Fire Priest. It is a collection of spells and charms to treat diseases.

FAST FACT

As per the Rigveda, the universe emerged from Prajapati, who is the earliest God and the creator of this world.

Palm leaf manuscript (top). Dried palm leaves were used as writing material in ancient India to record events, right from horoscopes to mythological stories (left).

Rise of Jainism

Statue of Jain god Gomeshvara in Shravanabelagola, India.

During the sixth century BCE, many great thinkers like Buddha, Mahavira, Heraclitus, Zoroaster, Confucius and Lao Tse propagated their ideas. The thinkers and their followers rose as one voice against orthodox religion, which followed rigid rituals and rites. Jainism also emerged due to the orthodox practices and rigid dogma of religion.

Time of social flux

It was a time of great social, political and intellectual flux when the old tribal structure of the society began to change. Some groups, known as republics, came into existence. The old social order began to slowly disintegrate and soon a conflict within religions arose. Further, many complicated rituals and sacrifices during the late Vedic period remained inaccessible to the common people and were also expensive. The beliefs confused many people and some of the teachings in the Upanishads were very philosophical, which could not be easily understood. All these factors led to disillusionment amongst the common people. They wanted a simple way towards salvation in a language that was known to them. Mahavira managed to do just that.

Caste system leading to rise of Jainism

Carvings in a Jain temple in Ranakpur, India.

Apart from the inaccessible religion, other equally important social and economic factors also gave rise to Jainism. One such factor was the caste system. The four castes were Brahmins, Kshatriyas, Vaishyas and the Shudras. The upper castes lived a life of privilege while the lower castes were discriminated against and denied many resources. This led to resentment against the upper castes. Mahavira belonged to the Kshatriya tribe. The Kshatriyas and Vaishyas wanted to improve their condition, but the rigid caste system denied them the chance. This led to the merchant class embracing Jainism.

Chaumukha Mandir–Jain Temple, Ranakpur, India.

Jain Tirthankaras

Jainism originated between the seventh and fifth centuries BCE. Followers of Jainism are known as Jains. Jainism does not have one founder, but 24 tirthankaras. The word tirthankara means a teacher who has surmounted the cycle of birth and death, and who shows others the path to attain moksh (salvation). The first tirthankara was Rishabhanatha. The 23rd Jain tirthankara was Parshvanatha. During the seventh century BCE, he developed a community based on the renouncement of worldly concerns.

Rockcut statue of Jain tirthankara in rock niches near Gwalior fort, India.

The one who leads

Parshvanatha was the 23rd tirthankara or the one who leads the way towards salvation. The twenty-fourth and final tirthankara was Vardhamana, also known as Mahavira (great hero). Mahavira was a contemporary of Gautam Buddha. Just like Buddha, Mahavira was a Kshatriya chieftain's son who renounced his princely status at the age of 30 to live the life of an ascetic. Mahavira spent around 12.5 years as a devout ascetic and attained enlightenment (kevalnyan).

He had 11 disciples or ganadharas. Of these disciples, Indrabhuti Gautama and Sudharman were the founders of the historical Jain monastic community. Mahavira is believed to have died at Pavapuri, near Patna.

A group of Digambar Jain nuns, sadhvis, attend a religious ceremony at a Jain temple.

Principles of Jainism

As per Jainism, right knowledge, right faith and right conduct can help a person attain moksha. For this, the five great vows—non-violence (ahimsa), truth (satya), non-stealing (asteya), celibacy (brahmacharya) and non-attachment (aparigraha)—should be followed.

Hutheesing Jain Temple, consecrated in 1848 AD, is one of the best known in Gujarat, India.

PROMINENT CIVILISATIONS

Rise of Buddhism

During the sixth century BCE, the Vedic religion had become orthodox and inflexible. An emphasis on expensive religious rituals made the common man feel disenchanted and alienated. The rigid caste system made the life of the people belonging to the lower castes miserable. Further, the religious texts were in Sanskrit, which the common people could not understand as they spoke Pali and Prakrit. This made the common man feel even more alienated. These factors helped in the rise of Buddhism.

Face of Buddha.

Buddhist monks praying.

A protected life

Buddhism is derived from the Hindi word "buddhi", meaning wisdom. Gautam Buddha was the founder of Buddhism. His real name was Siddhartha and he was a prince. Born into a royal family in Lumbini, as a child Siddhartha was protected from all negative things in the world. However, one day after leaving the royal household, Siddhartha saw—an old man, a sick man, a corpse and a monk, for the first time. He realised that old age, sickness and death were a part of human life.

Becoming the Buddha

He renounced his kingdom to seek answers as to why there is so much sorrow and pain, why people age and how one can get rid of his or her sorrows and pain.

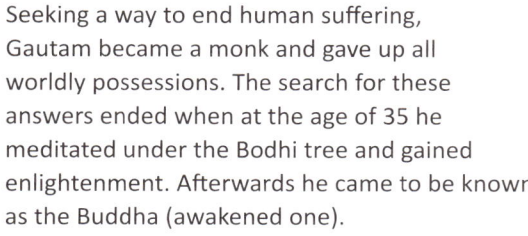

Thai Buddhist monk.

Seeking a way to end human suffering, Gautam became a monk and gave up all worldly possessions. The search for these answers ended when at the age of 35 he meditated under the Bodhi tree and gained enlightenment. Afterwards he came to be known as the Buddha (awakened one).

First sermon at Sarnath

Five weeks after attaining enlightenment, Gautam Buddha travelled to Sarnath where he delivered his first sermon to five monks, teaching them what he had learnt. This was the beginning of the Buddhist sangha or community of monks. Over the next 40 years, Gautam Buddha travelled around north India to spread his teachings.

Young Buddhist novices pray at Shwezigon Pagoda near Bagan.

FAST FACT

Gautam Buddha's wife Yashodhara and son Rahula also joined the Buddhist sangha or monastic community.

21

Principles of Buddhism

Buddhism aims to achieve nirvana by following the path laid down by Gautam Buddha. Buddhists don't believe in a personal god. Karma, or action, is an important element of Buddhism. It is believed that if we do good in this life, we will have a better life when we are reborn. Although Buddhism originated in India, it presently has more followers in countries like Thailand, Japan and China.

Red and golden Buddha statue.

Tibetan prayer wheels in a Buddhist temple.

Tibetan buddhist Mani wheel or hand prayer wheel.

Four noble truths of Buddhism

Buddhism revolves around the four noble truths: (1) suffering, (2) origin or cause of suffering, (3) cessation of suffering and (4) the path to the cessation of suffering. The Buddha prescribed the eightfold path that to end suffering. It includes right views, right intention, right speech, right action, right livelihood, right effort, right concentration and right mindfulness.

Reason behind the noble truths

In the first two noble truths, Buddha diagnosed the problem (suffering) and identified its cause (desire). The third noble truth is the realisation that there is a cure to human suffering. The fourth noble truth is a prescription or detailed method through which humans can achieve a release from suffering.

The Middle Path

In his first sermon at Sarnath, Buddha called the Eightfold Path as the Middle Path because it prescribes a life of moderation, a middle way between the two extremes of austere asceticism and indulgence of desires.

The different colours of the lotus represent the different stages of the spiritual journey.

FAST FACT

The pink lotus is the supreme lotus, which is generally reserved for the enlightened one or Buddha. The white lotus symbolises the Bodhi or the awakened state.

Spread of Buddha's Word

Old Buddhist Temple Wat Yai Chai Mongkhon in Ayutthaya Province, Thailand.

King Ashoka was a follower of Buddhism and played an important role in the spread of this religion. He used oral announcements to spread Buddha's teachings and also had them inscribed on rocks and pillars at various sites, such as Sarnath.

Ashokan pillar with four Asiatic lions on top.

Impact of the Kalinga War

After fighting a brutal war to conquer Kalinga in the third century BCE, Ashoka felt deep remorse when he saw the bloodshed and destruction caused by the war. Consequently, he denounced any form of violence. Ashoka became a devout follower of Buddha and vowed to follow the path of non-violence or ahimsa.

Ashoka and Buddhism

Ashoka himself practised Buddhism, but he respected his people's wishes and gave them the freedom to follow the religion of their choice.

He undertook tours to preach Buddhist philosophy and also asked his officers to participate. He built hospitals for people and animals, planted trees along the roads and gave orders to reduce taxes and prevent cruelty to animals.

The Buddhist council

Ashoka organised the Third Buddhist council and supported Buddhist missions that travelled as far as Greece, Egypt and Syria.

There is a mention in the Buddhist Theravada tradition of a group of Buddhist missionaries who were sent by Emperor Ashoka to a Buddhist school in Sri Lanka in 240 BCE.

Due to his efforts, the religion gained prominence, particularly after he made Buddhism his state religion. Thus, Ashoka helped to spread Buddhism far and wide.

262–261 BCE: Kalinga war

250 BCE: Placing of the Lion capital in Sarnath

Great Stupa (ancient Buddhist monument) in Sanchi, Madhya Pradesh, India.

HISTORY ENCYCLOPEDIA

The Mauryan Dynasty

Alexander's campaign in northwest India lasted from 327 to 325 BCE. A few years later, in 321 BCE, Chandragupta Maurya founded the Mauryan dynasty.

Temple 18 and the Great Stupa (Stupa 1) at Sanchi.

Mauryan empire

After Alexander's death, Chandragupta Maurya, the founder of the Mauryan dynasty, created an empire that would go on to cover most of India. However, this did not include present-day Tamil Nadu. The empire had a well-organised army and civil service. Chandragupta was assisted by his advisor Chanakya, who was a teacher at Takshashila. Chanakya authored the treatise Arthashashtra that explains the duties of a king, methods to manage the economy and administration of the Mauryan empire and steps to maintain law and order.

Statue of Chandragupta Maurya.

Ashoka the Great

The Buddhist Mauryan emperor Ashoka ruled from 265 to 238 BCE. He was the third ruler of the Mauryan empire, which was the largest empire in the Indian subcontinent. After the Kalinga war, Ashoka maintained friendly relations with his neighbouring kingdoms.

He worked towards extending Buddhism and spreading Buddhist teachings across the world. He commissioned some of the finest works of ancient Indian art. He built several Buddhist monuments, such as stupas, sangharama, viharas and chaityas. Ashoka set up clinics for people and animals, and had wells dug out for the benefit of his people. Further, he abolished hunting and fishing. After Ashoka's death, the Mauryan empire began to decline. Brihadratha was the last Mauryan ruler, who was assassinated 50 years after Ashoka's death.

Ashokan lion pillar at Vaishali in India.

FAST FACT

Ashoka in Sanskrit means "the one without sorrow". He was also known as Chakravartin Samraat, or the emperor of emperors and sometimes as Priyadarshin, or the one who looks at everyone with love.

Chandragupta Maurya and his bride from Babylon.

PROMINENT CIVILISATIONS

Persian Empire

The Persian Empire rose in Western Asia after the fall of the Babylonian Empire. Lasting less than 250 years, it was the largest empire in the ancient world.

Stone bas-relief of Persian soldiers in Persepolis, Iran.

FAST FACT

The name "Persian" comes from the tribal name "Parsua". This was the name given to the land surrounded by the Tigris River where the Persians originally settled.

Cyrus the Great

The Achaemenid Empire was founded by Cyrus the Great. His name was derived from Kuros, meaning "like the sun". He founded Persia by uniting the Medes and the Persians - two original Iranian tribes. He then went on to conquer the Lydians and the Babylonians. Under his rule, the people were allowed to practise a religion of their choice. They could keep their customs as long as they paid taxes and obeyed the rulers.

The Great Cylinder

Cyrus the Great was known for creating the first Charter of Human Rights known to humankind. It was written on a clay cylinder, which was excavated in 1879 by an Assyro-British archaeologist called Hormuzd Rassam. It is said that the script on the cylinder was written by Cyrus himself. It was written in the Akkadian language with a cuneiform script. Passages in the text express the emperor's humanity, religious tolerance and freedom. Today, Cyrus the Great is remembered as a wise, peaceful leader and a liberator of his people.

Fighting the Greeks

After the death of Cyrus the Great, the next strong emperor to come into power was Darius I. Under his rule, the Persians tried to expand their empire by conquering Greece. King Darius first attacked Greece in 490 BCE. However, he only managed to conquer a few city-states, before he was defeated at Athens. His dream of conquering Greece was fulfilled by his son Xerxes I in 480 BCE when he won the Battle of Thermopylae against a strong army of Spartans.

Ruins of the city of Persepolis, the capital of the Persian Empire.

The Cyrus Cylinder, now preserved at the British museum, London.

HISTORY ENCYCLOPEDIA

The Vikings: A Warrior Civilisation

Large numbers of Scandinavian seafaring warriors raided and colonized several settlements between the eighth and eleventh centuries. These warriors were known as Vikings or Norsemen. For three centuries, they made their mark on large parts of England, Europe, Russia, Iceland, Greenland and Newfoundland.

It is a popular misconception that Vikings wore helmets with two horns when in fact their helmets were likely made of iron or leather.

Landowners and farmers take to the sea

The Vikings basically comprised heads of clans or landowners who were in search of adventure and loot. On their own lands, they were farmers, but once they set out, they turned into violent raiders and pillagers. Thus, power-hungry chieftains would organise bands of armies, set forth on longships and raid coastal cities and towns, plundering, burning, and killing at will.

Longships were seagoing vessels used by the Vikings for their seafaring adventures.

Making inroads into England and Europe

By the middle of the ninth century, the Vikings had made significant inroads into Ireland, Scotland and England. They brought much of Scotland under their control; they established Ireland's early trading towns of Dublin, Waterford, Wexford, Wicklow and Limerick. Only the kingdom of Wessex withstood the Vikings.

Turning their attention to Europe, the Vikings took advantage of Europe's internal conflicts, realising that many European rulers were willing to pay richly to keep the Vikings away from attacking their subjects. They attacked and occupied large parts of France (the name Normandy comes from The Land of the Northmen), Italy, Denmark, Greenland and Iceland.

PROMINENT CIVILISATIONS

The Viking legacy

Even though the Viking age ended over nine centuries ago, some legacies of the Norse civilisation remain. The Viking society believed in law and democracy. The "Althing" was believed to be Europe's first national assembly, with powers akin to parliament. Though women could not vote, they did enjoy tremendous equality, running farms and businesses while their husbands were at sea. They could inherit property and even initiate divorce.

The Viking age was also known for its art forms and craft. The Vikings wrote with a set of alphabets called "runes". The Vikings also appeared to have high hygienic standards, as is evident from excavations of tweezers, razors, ear cleaners and combs that were made from bones. The importance of boats in the Viking way of life is evident from the fact that sometimes they buried their dead on boats or wagons.

FAST FACT
The Vikings considered swords as their most precious possession and even gave them names like "Fierce" or "Leg biter".

Famous Vikings

Rollo—First ruler of Normandy
He was either of Danish or Norwegian origin and raided France in the tenth century.

Erik the Red
He was possibly called so due to his red hair and fiery temper. He set his sights and conquered Greenland.

Olaf Tryggvason
Great-grandson of Viking leader Harald I Fairhair, Olaf led a Viking attack on England. He forced his subjects to convert to Christianity. In 1000, he was defeated and is believed to have jumped over the side of his ship.

Leif Eriksson
Son of Erik the Red, he is believed to have landed in North America much before Columbus. However, he was unable to establish himself successfully.

Cnut the Great
He was the son of Denmark's King Sweyn Forkbeard. He helped his father conquer England in 1013.

Harald (Hardrada) Sigurdsson
He led 300 ships to challenge William the Conqueror and gain control of Northern England. He was killed at the battle of York. "Hardrada" means hard ruler.

Chinese Civilisation

Ancient China is one of the oldest civilisations of the world. Its history can be traced back to over 7000 years. Like the Indus Valley Civilisation, the Chinese civilisation was cut out from the rest of the world—as it was bounded by oceans, mountains and deserts—making it inaccessible to outsiders. Being cut off from others gave rise to a feeling of nationalism among the Chinese. They believed themselves to be the strongest empire, ruled by powerful families called dynasties. The first recorded Chinese dynasty was the Shang Dynasty, which is said to have ruled China from 1766 to 1122 BCE.

Portrait of Emperor Qianlong of the Qing dynasty, the last dynasty to rule China.

Mongols and the Great Wall

The Mongols were the greatest enemy of the Chinese, frequently attacking them from the north. To keep the Mongols from invading, the Chinese built a huge wall, stretching for miles on its northern border. Started by the Qin dynasty, the wall continued to be built by the dynasties that followed. Most of the wall, as we see it today, was built by the Ming dynasty. It is the longest man-made structure in the world, stretching up to 8900 km. The wall also had towers, where soldiers would stand to keep guard.

Chinese technology and inventions

The Chinese are known for their inventions. They invented silk and paper. Printing was first practised in ancient China on wooden blocks. Their other inventions include gunpowder, crossbows, hand fans, fireworks, ploughs, kites, harnesses, umbrellas, wheelbarrows, paper money, the compass, the abacus and the Grand Canal.

The wheelbarrow was invented by the Chinese.

The Great Wall of China.

PROMINENT CIVILISATIONS

Traditional Chinese medicine

Medicine in China was developed almost 5000 years ago. They devised various healing methods, many of which are still in use. Some of these are acupuncture or the science of healing through needles pierced at critical points; acupressure or the science of healing by applying pressure at key points; and herbs made from thousands of medicinal plants or even dried animals parts.

Needles are used for acupuncture.

Languages in China

There are many languages and dialects in China, which are known as Sinitic languages. The main language group, Chinese Han, comes from the Sino-Tibetan area. Other languages are Mandarin, Wu, Gan, Hakka, Xiang and Cantonese. The languages differ in grammar, vocabulary and pronunciation. Today, Modern Standard Chinese has been accepted as one of the six official languages by the United Nations as an outcome of a programme for the unification of the national language, based on Mandarin.

Calligraphy is a known art in China with elaborate and delicate strokes creating virtual pieces of art.

The history of Chinese cuisine

Chinese food is among the most popular cuisines in the world. The importance of food in Chinese ancient culture dates back to the days of the emperor. Chefs were in high demand. Yi Yin, Prime Minister in the seventeenth century, began his life as a cook. Typically, food was cut into small pieces before being cooked, so that it cooked fast. This was primarily because of low fuel supply. Each area of China had a distinct style of cooking and ingredients differed based on local availability. In northern China, wheat was used for noodles and dumplings; whereas in the south, there was a greater prevalence of rice.

The Chinese Terracotta warriors

Ying Zheng became an Emperor at the age of 13 in 246 BCE. Over the next several years, he unified a number of warring kingdoms and became the first Emperor of Qin dynasty. A lot of achievements like the standardisation of coins, weights, measures, building of canals and roads, etc., are attributed to him. He commissioned the creation of an army of terracotta warriors to accompany him into the afterlife. Over 700,000 workers were involved in the creation of the famous Terracotta Warrior Army. Archeologists excavated four pits that were filled with terracotta soldiers, weapons and horsedrawn chariots. The fourth pit remains empty, suggesting that the task was never completed. There are estimated to be over 6000 soldiers. These give us an idea of the life, army, clothes and social structure of that time.

The Chinese eat sticky rice with chopsticks even today.

The army of terracotta warriors was intended to serve the emperor in the afterlife.

A terracotta horsedrawn carriage as a part of the terracotta army.

The Dynasties of China

Ancient China was ruled by 13 main dynasties for over 3000 years.

1. **Xia dynasty** – Considered to be the first dynasty in ancient China, it lasted for nearly 500 years under the rule of 17 emperors.

2. **Shang dynasty** – This dynasty lasted for 600 years and was ruled by 30 emperors. It was also known as the Yin dynasty.

3. **Chou (Zhou) dynasty** – This dynasty was founded by Wuwang. It was the longest dynasty and saw 37 emperors over 800 years.

4. **Qin dynasty** – It came into power in 221 BCE, ruling for only 15 years.

5. **Han dynasty** – It ruled from about 206 BCE to 220 CE and was a period of peace and prosperity.

6. **The Six Dynasties rule** – During this rule, six smaller dynasties held power for the next three and a half centuries. These were:
   - Wu (222 CE–280 CE)
   - Dong (Eastern) Jin (317 CE–420 CE)
   - Liu-Song (420 CE–479 CE)
   - Nan (Southern) Qi (479 CE–502 CE)
   - Nan Liang (502 CE–557 CE)
   - Nan Chen (557 CE–589 CE)

7. **Sui dynasty** – Lasted for only 38 years during which the Great Wall of China was built.

8. **Tang dynasty** – Also known as the Golden Age of Ancient China, this dynasty saw the rise of arts, literature and technology. It ended in 907 CE.

9. **Five Dynasties** – This was a period of 53 years, when five specific dynasties held sway. These were:
   - Later Liang Dynasty
   - Later Tang Dynasty
   - Later Jin Dynasty
   - Later Han Dynasty
   - Later Zhou Dynasty

10. **Song dynasty** – It was founded by General Zhao Kuangyin in the 960s by unifying many warring kingdoms.

11. **Yuan dynasty** – Also known as the Mongol dynasty, this dynasty was founded by Mongol nomads.

12. **Ming dynasty** – It was the last of the great Chinese dynasties and it came into power after it overthrew the Mongols.

13. **Qing dynasty** – It was set up by the Manchus, who invaded China in 1644 CE and overthrew the last Ming emperor.

A porcelain vase from the Ming dynasty.

FAST FACT

The name China was most probably derived from the name Qin (pronounced as Chin) dynasty.

PROMINENT CIVILISATIONS

The Inca Civilisation

Considered to be one of the largest in pre-Columbian America, the Inca civilisation came into being during the twelfth century. The Incas took over large parts of Western South America; sometimes through peaceful methods but often through violent conquests. The land was combined into a state almost as large as some of Eurasia's historical empires. Having made Cuzco (now Peru) their capital in the twelfth century, within a hundred years, the Incas brought almost twelve million people in the region under their control.

Inca icon

Expanding boundaries

It is believed that Manco Capac, the earliest known leader of the Inca tribe, settled his tribe in Cuzco. It was under the fourth emperor, Mayta Capac, that the Inca began to truly expand their influence. They plundered neighbouring villages and brought them under their control. Over the succeeding generations, the Incas established themselves in a position of superiority.

It was during the reign of Topa Inca Yupanqui (1471–93) that the Inca empire was the most widespread. When he died, there was a struggle for succession and Huayna Capac (1493–1525) came to power. Huayna Capac further extended the northern boundary of the empire, but his death brought about another succession struggle. This remained unresolved when the Spanish arrived in Peru in 1532. By 1535, the Inca civilisation came to an end.

Advanced architecture

At the helm of the Inca society was the emperor, who ruled ruthlessly and harshly with the help of an aristocratic bureaucracy. Technology and architecture during this period were fairly advanced. Excavations have unearthed evidence of fortifications, places of worship, palaces and irrigation systems from this period.

Inca's water canal in the archeological site of Ollantaytambo, Sacred Valley, a major travel destination in the Cuzco region of Peru. Inca terraces can be seen in the background.

Machu Picchu, an Inca site built during the fifteenth century, is a World Heritage Site. It means "Old Peak".

The Inca economy was primarily agricultural, with a predominance of crops like maize, potatoes, peanuts, cocoa, cassava, cotton, etc. Domestic animals were raised and utilised in farms. Clothing was largely made of llama wool, as well as cotton.

The Inca religion

The Incas worshipped animals and nature gods. Inti, the Sun God; Apu Illapu, the rain God; and Viracocha, the God of creation were among the chief Gods they worshipped. They conducted elaborate rituals that included both animal and human sacrifice. Many of these rituals were discontinued after the Spanish conquest.

The Incas believed that the Earth, the moon, the stars and the Sun were all created by the God Viracocha. The legend claimed that he plucked them from an island in the middle of Lake Titicaca. The official ruler of the Incas was said to be Sapa Inca, which meant "Son of the Sun". The high priests chose women to serve the religion. Girls were sometimes chosen when they were very young. These girls or women were called "acllas".

Ancient Inca circular terraces suggest organised farming.

Evidence of the advanced architectural abilities of the Incas lies in the vast road network they built. Not much is left of the original Inca culture today. However, their lineage seems to have been carried forward by the peasants living on the Andes, who are believed to be descendants of the Inca. The peasants speak a language called Quechua and account for almost 45 per cent of Peru's population. Primarily farmers, they follow a version of Roman Catholicism with a pagan hierarchy.

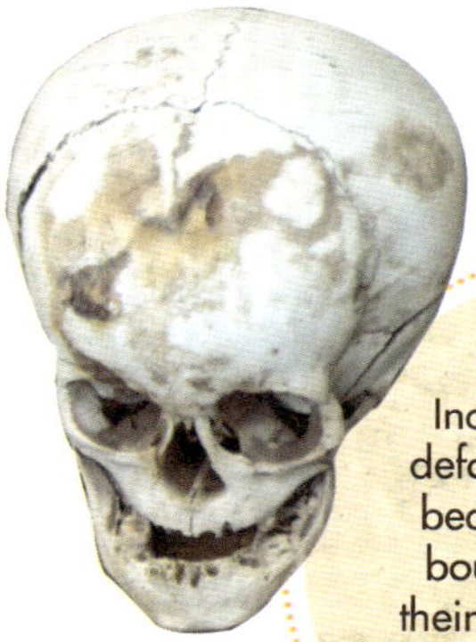

A sacrificial ceremonial axe made of either wood, bronze or copper.

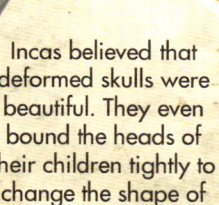

FAST FACT

Incas believed that deformed skulls were beautiful. They even bound the heads of their children tightly to change the shape of their skull.

View of the ancient Inca City of Machu Picchu, often called the "Lost city of the Incas".